port

Neil Mathieson

CHARTWELL
BOOKS, INC.

This edition published in 1999 by
CHARTWELL BOOKS, INC.
A division of BOOK SALES, INC
114 Northfield Avenue,
Edison, New Jersey 08837

Produced by
PRC Publishing Ltd,
Kiln House, 210 New Kings Road, London SW6 4NZ

© 1999 PRC Publishing Ltd.

ISBN 0 78581 059 5

Printed and bound in Hong Kong

Glossary

Aguardente	The fortifying grape spirit or brandy
Colheita	Vintage
Hectare	land measurement of 10,000 square metres or approximately 2.47 acres
I.V.P.	Instituto do Vinho do Porto
Lodge	The building used for storage and maturation
Pipe	The commonly used cask size, 580-630 litres (153-166 U.S. gallons)
Quinta	Vineyard estate or farm

Written by Neil Mathieson, Managing Director of Eaux de Vie Ltd, the
U.K.'s leading independent spirit shipper and importer of fine Ports.

Acknowledgements

Thanks to all the port houses who have helped in the research, partic-
ular thanks go to Tim Stanley-Clarke and others at the Symington
Group, Jorge Rosas of Ramos Pinto, Paul Gow of Burmester and
Joanna Delaforce and Maria Emilia Campos of Churchill Graham, Sue
Glasgow of The Port Wine Institute in London and Corlos Moreira of
the IVP in Oporto. To the various UK trade publications such as
Harpers Wine & Spirit Gazette and *Wine & Spirit International* who
have kept me up to date with the latest happenings in Portugal and
also to all those who supplied labels, pictures — particularly the
Instituto do Vinho do Porto, in Portugal — for providing many of the
pictures and of course the many samples provided for photography
and tasting.

Additional information has been gathered over twenty years of
discussion and tasting, both willingly supplied by my many colleagues
in the wine trade, and to the friends for whom my own cellar has provided the bottles for many post-dinner discourses.

Contents

Introduction

THE REGION

Port is a fortified wine produced from grapes grown alongside the upper reaches of the Duoro River and its tributaries, in northern Portugal. The river flows from its mouth at Oporto, on the Atlantic coastline, through Portugal to the Spanish border. Even before other European countries had considered demarcating the areas from within which their most famous products would be produced, the Portuguese had delimited the production region for port wines. In fact the Upper Duoro vineyard area was proscribed in 1756, the first

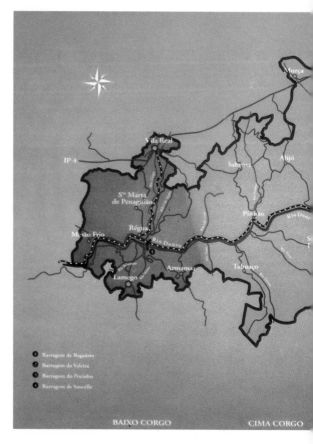

vineyard area to be controlled so, anywhere. The area is approximately 750,000 acres (300,00ha) in size and is ringed by granite hills.

The soil types and the individual microclimates found from valley to valley, as one follows the river, have been the guidelines for the sub-zones that make up the vineyard areas. The finest vineyards start in earnest when the River Corgo meets the Duoro at Régua where the natural granite hills are interrupted by schistous soils on either side of the river.

The first planted region is called the Baixo, or lower Corgo, and has the lowest temperatures and the most rainfall of the three zones. The river banks here are not so steep, the vines heavily cultivated, and the growth more abundant. This allows for heavier cropping of lighter wines without the potential backbone that is required for the best ports. Although it acccounts for around a quarter of the vineyard area, the Baixo Corgo has almost half of the whole region's vineyards and is vital in the production of the big-selling everyday ports.

The zone from Régua to just after the River Tau is known as the Cima Corgo and here is the heart of the production area, where most of the famous quintas, or farms, such as Malvedos,

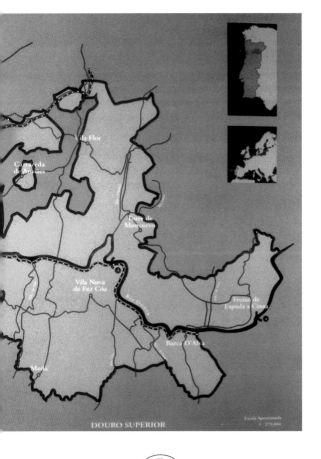

Nova, and Roêda are situated. Around the town of Pinhão the hillsides are steeper, the terraces shallower, and the climate hotter and drier. The vines, working commensurably harder, produce more concentration in the grape and thus more weight and flavor in the wine.

As we head towards Spain, the area is known as the Duoro Superior and farms here are bigger with fewer terraces and more mechanization. Here the famous quintas of Vargellas, Vesúvio, and further to the east, Ramos Pinto's Ervamoira are to be found. The most arid of the regions, the Duoro Superior, nevertheless produces wines which many shippers use in their premium ports, although only supplying about 5% of the total wine used for port production.

THE VINEYARD AND VINES

Due to the dramatic contours of the Duoro Valley, the majority of vineyards are situated on terraces, allowing the sun unhindered access to the vine. The terraces have developed from those supported by brick walls and carrying only a single or double row of vines to wider *patamares*, or terraces, with earth banks that can carry more rows and which allow access for small tractors. Where the slopes are gentler the vines can often follow the hills, like a carpet, giving greater productivity.

The vineyards are graded by an intricate points' system, which to the outsider may seem quite arcane. The vineyard will earn positive or negative points for four major factors — low altitude, low yields, schistous soils, and pre-marked localities — and eight minor factors — vine training, grape varieties, slope, aspect, soil stoniness, the age of the vines, and the degree of shelter of the vineyard. Once the factors have been calculated the vineyard is then rated from the best, grade A, to the lowliest, grade F, and upon this score rests the beneficio.

The beneficio is set by the Instituto do Vinho do Porto, the governing body, and gives the limit, in litres of grape must per vine, that the different grades of vineyard may fortify, each harvest, to make port wine. The wine itself can be red or white and retains a natural sweetness when the fermentation process is stopped by the addition of native grape brandy (*aguardente*). The use of the term Port or Porto for wine is nowadays subject to the limitations

The Duoro Valley is characterised by its terraces, whose schistous soil allows the roots of the vines to penetrate deeply (as far as 30m down) to gain nutrients — necessary in the desert conditions of summer.

above, although this has only recently been accepted internationally, and is a very valuable tool for   marketing the unique properties of these wines throughout the world.

Like most of the other European vineyard areas, the Duoro was hard hit by the phyloxera epidemic in the later years of the 19th century and almost all vines are now grafted onto American root stocks. Common practice, vineyard legend has it, used to dictate that each cut stem was placed in the mouth of the grafter and anointed with local wine, before joining with the root stock, to ensure that the graft took.

The vines themselves can only be described as a mixed bag! It is not unknown for a Duoro farmer to have more than 20 varieties side by side in one vineyard and to not know the offi-cially recognized names for more than half of them. From the Touriga Nacional, Touriga Francesa, Tinta Cão, Tinta Barroca, and Tinta Roriz which are widely respected as the great port grapes to the lesser known and more esoterically named Borrado das Moscas (fly droppings) and Esgana Cão (dog strangler) there are more than 80 red and white varieties grown in the Douro, of which more than 40 are acceptable for port production.

Recent work, carried out with the support of the World Bank and the EU, has started to unravel the viticultural knot, but more work and planting still remains to be done. Pruning and wire training are also being studied with the best grapes planted in plots together and the best training methods for each grape variety utilized.

A BRIEF HISTORY

The first great increase in vine planting, in the Duoro region, took place in the early 1600s and then again between 1678 and 1697 when the British further influenced the production of wine by placing an embargo on French imports. When this embargo was lifted, at the turn of the 18th century, duties on French wines were double those on Portuguese, and the British share of wine exported during the following century reached almost 90%. This preference of the British was cemented in 1703 by treaty and it was during the next 100 years that many of the first great port shipping houses, such as Warre's, Croft's and C. N. Kopke

finally established permanent offices to trade in wine.

Further growth of the wine industry was greatly hindered by the expansion of the Portuguese Empire and soon domestic agriculture was facing a crisis, which was solved by the establishment of a national board of trade to take control of the Duoro wine trade. This was followed, in 1727, by the founding of the British shippers' association and in 1755 by the founding of the Oporto Wine Company which, after a few false starts, eventually standardized the production, the level of fortification with brandy, and the shape and size of the bottle. Finally, in 1786 the Factory House of the British Association was built and this became the de facto chamber of commerce for the English shipping houses.

Both the French Revolution and the Peninsular War greatly disrupted the port wine trade, but following this and through the efforts of, amongst others, the Marquis of Pombal and Baron Forrester, the vineyard areas were fully mapped and production methods

The terraces are the result of centuries of work, and it is the combination of their soil, rich in phosphorous, and the intense summer heat that produces grapes of remarkable concentration.

laid down on paper for all to study. All through the 18th century the shippers and growers faced regulatory problems with the Government who, of course, objected to foreign companies making so much profit out of one of Portugal's prime exports as well as the tragedy of the phyloxera epidemic of 1868, and then in this century, the difficulties associated with two world wars.

The port trade has also been unable to avoid the predatory eyes of the large wine and spirit producing multinationals. Allied Domecq, Diageo through its ID subsidiary, Seagram, and Louis Vuitton-Moët Hennessy have all bought port shippers and these, with the Portuguese giants Sogrape, Barros Almeida, and Royal Oporto, now vie with the remaining traditional large English companies, the Symington Group and the Taylor/Fonseca combine, for the majority of export sales.

These export markets have also changed in the last 40 years: long gone are the days when the United Kingdom was the largest buyer of port wine. Now the biggest markets are France with its preference for younger wines for aperitif drinking and the Benelux countries that favor aged tawnies. Premium ports are still the favorite of the UK and the United States, with America now importing more vintage-dated ports than any other country.

PORT PRODUCTION

The late summer is vital and if the weather is good, and the vineyards have avoided any problems, then by late September the grapes are ready for harvesting.

Picking of the grapes takes place by hand, with the loaded baskets being carried or trucked to the winery where they are either trodden whole in a granite lagar or crushed, destemmed, and pumped into the fermenting tanks.

Traditionally, the finest ports are always foot-trodden, but as these make up a relatively small proportion of the total production most of the wine is made in tank. The granite troughs or lagares are mostly between 1,300 and 2,100 gallons (5,000 and 8,000 litres) in size and treading starts as soon as the vineyard workers have eaten in the evening. The first treading session, the corte, lasts for two to three hours with the treaders methodically marching back

Towards the middle of September, the ripe grapes are plucked from the vines. This rich harvest traditionally went to the lagares, open granite tanks where it was trod to release the juice and allow fermentation. Today the grapes are more likely to end up in stainless steel fermenting tanks.

and forwards; then the liberdade is announced and the dancing can begin — often to drums and accordion music. After about five hours the grape must has warmed up, the natural yeasts on the skins have started to react, and fermentation has begun; now at long last the dancers can leave the lagare. During the rest of the fermentation period the crown of skins is continually pushed back into the bubbling must and an alcoholic degree of about 5% is achieved before the juice is run off.

Of course, with the vast majority of port heading for the lighter ruby and tawny styles, more economic, although unfortunately less romantic, ways of crushing the grapes have been developed and two tank methods are used. The grapes processed this way are crushed and partially destemmed, and then pumped into the fermenting tanks. The closed tank system incorporates a self-circulating autovinification method, which comes into play when the fermentation begins. The pressure caused by the production of carbon dioxide allows a water-based valve system to re-circulate the fermenting juice and extract the flavor and color from the grapes.

The open tank method involves pumping the must from under the cap up and over the floating skins at regular intervals. The extraction of the color and tannins from the grape skins is of vital importance for a wine whose fermentation is short yet whose life is expected to be long.

Once the half-fermented wine has reached the appropriate sugar and alcohol balance it is run off into casks where the fortifying grape brandy lies, the remaining skins and pulp are pressed and the resultant juice blended in with the free run. The high strength brandy or aguardente stops the fermentation in its tracks and leaves the resulting wine naturally sweet. A proportion of about 1:4 of brandy is used which leaves the port at an alcoholic degree of between 15 and 17%. The wines are then stored in bulk and racked for the first time in the early spring to take away the dead yeast cells and other sediments.

Now comes the time when the cellar masters and blenders must decide on the future of their wine. Already, following the picking, pressing, and fermentation, they will have an excellent idea of the potential of the wines. The decision will be made on which

The young port stays in the vineyard for its first winter before being brought down to the coast where the humidity and temperature is better for maturation. In the low lodges — armazéns — the port matures in casks called pipas — pipes. It is tasted regularly by experts to assess its quality.

batches are to be used for blending and ageing as young ruby or tawny, or be selected for ageing in oak casks known as pipes for premium and vintage dated wines.

ABOUT THE WINES

One can divide the styles of port made, in several different ways — by color, length of time in bottle as opposed to cask, or those that are dated with the vintage year or undated. The Instituto do Vinho do Porto gives us nine different types that are recognized and these cover almost all the styles commercially available.

White Port
Made from white grapes, white port ranges from young light styles, which are an interesting aperitif, to those deeper in color and age. Both can be made in dry or sweet styles but the most elegant are the slightly drier styles that have had up to ten years in cask, such as Churchill's which is actually labeled as White Porto Dry Aperitif.

Ruby
Young, medium to full-bodied wines which have spent about three years in wood. The wines have a bright ruby red color and a youthful lively spicy sweet flavor. This is the biggest category of port sales and good quality ruby has an invigorating uncomplicated forthright flavor, but some of the lesser wines can be slightly coarse and unknit.

Vintage Character
These are blended ports of about four years of age. The wines must have had the initial characteristics of vintage ports and be of good quality but today they tend to have been filtered and are ready for bottling on release. Cockburn's Vintage Character Special Reserve is the world's biggest seller in this category and the Fonseca "Bin 27" is at the least an equal to the best with its fine structure and consistency.

Tawny
A huge category that covers all wood aged ports blended from a number of harvests. Ageing in cask can be anything from three years to more than 40, and the wines over time lose their deep color and take on a smooth

nutty flavor with a reddy brown color. As the wines age they are often blended and the stated ages that are marketed — 10, 20, 30, and over 40 become the average age much as those offered by solera sherries in Spain. Burmester, Neipoort, and Ramos Pinto all make excellent 10-20 year old tawnies and Taylor's a great 40-year old.

Late Bottled Vintage

Port from a single good harvest, bottled after spending a minimum of five years and a maximum of six years in cask. The wines are more complex than the premium rubies but are softer and more approachable than a full vintage. Two styles are offered — the traditional LBV that will throw a sediment and therefore develops further in bottle and will need decanting, and wines that have been filtered and are immediately ready for drinking. Smith Woodhouse, Ramos Pinto, and Warre's make good traditional LBV; Quinta de la Rosa, Taylor's, and Graham's provide the best of the more modern type.

Crusted

This is a small category, in the past much beloved of the regular vintage port drinker. Crusted ports are a blend of fine wines from a number of harvests, which are bottled without being filtered and then laid down to mature like vintage wines. The wine will naturally throw a crust or sediment and therefore needs decanting. Using this method, good rich full flavored wines can be made and offered at a lower price than the single quinta or vintage declarations. The date on a bottle of crusted port is that of bottling. Often made only by the smaller English shippers, these wines can offer very good value.

VINTAGE WINES

Single Quinta Vintages

These are ports from a single harvest, from an individual farm or Quinta. They are bottled like a full vintage and will mature further in bottle. Although the staple vintage product of the individual houses offering only their own quinta product, these wines are used by the larger shippers to fill the gaps between vintages and tend to be offered on the market when ready to drink, although many will continue to age

port

well. Almost all the large shippers now offer a single quinta wine and the individual farms to look out for are Crasto, de la Rosa, Infantado, and the Symington's Vesúvio.

Colheita

These are single harvest tawnies made from particularly high quality wines and they must be aged in wood for a minimum of seven years. In order to make clear the difference between these wines and full declared vintages the label must state that the port has been aged in wood, the year of the harvest, and the year of bottling. A speciality of the Portuguese houses, many of these wines can have a distinctively nutty flavor and a rich dried fruit finish, some names to look out for are Krohn, Feist, and Cálem.

Full Vintage Declarations

The most famous category, although in real terms only a very small percentage of wine is ever declared as a full vintage. What makes a vintage port is a simple question to answer — the wines must be of a single harvest and be bottled between July 1 of the second year and June 30 of the third year, following harvest. What makes a great vintage is another question.

The proposed vintage wines are selected following fermentation and then aged for up to a year, samples are then sent to the IVP with figures for the quantity of wine, its provenance, and the proposed release details. When the shippers receive approval that the wines will be granted the IVP's seal of guarantee, then the market conditions will be studied, the other shippers consulted, and possibly a vintage declared. Because these wines represent the pinnacle of the shipper's range, their reputation is often tied to the performance of their vintages — in some cases less than 1% of the wine they actually make. It is brave house that does not follow the other houses in excellent years or that declares wines that they are not fully confident of. Unfortunately, this does not mean that every declaration is as good as the next or that each house's wines will be of similar excellent quality.

Many evenings have been spent and many bottles consumed discussing the merits of one vintage over another and one house versus the next, but because of the vagaries of the micro-

climate within the production area and the differences in wine making and house styles I am sure that these discussions will remain part of the mystique of vintage port for years to come.

PROMINENT DECLARED VINTAGES

I have split these into three age groups, and where some houses produced very fine wines in undervalued or not generally declared years:

Almost ancient history!

1908   Widely declared.

1912   Shipped by almost everyone.

1920   Widely declared.

1924   Small but excellent wines; especially Taylor's.

1927   Widely declared; fine wines from Cockburn's, Fonseca, Taylor's, and Noval.

1931   Not generally declared; superb concentrated wines from Noval and Niepoort.

1934/5   Split between the shippers; Fonseca and Noval good in 1934, Cockburn and Taylor in 1935.

1945   Almost everyone; bottled in Oporto and superb from Taylor's, Graham's, and Dow's.

1947/8   Small quantities but fine wines; Cockburn, Sandeman, and Warre's in 1947 and Taylor's, Graham's, and Fonseca stand out in 1948.

1955   Almost every-one; Cockburn's, Graham's, and Taylor's excelled.

Still alive and ageing well!

1963   A classic and just coming round; superb wines from Cockburn's, Croft's, Fonseca, Taylor's, at the moment, and can be cellared for many more years.

1966   Widely declared; a little overshadowed by the 1963 but Fonseca, Dow's, and Noval's Nacional are great wines.

1970   Almost everyone; look out for Cálem, Delaforce, and Martinez amongst the less well known and big wines from Niepoort, Noval, and Taylor's.

1975   Widely declared; light wines for drinking now, stay with Dow's,

p o r t

Fonseca, and Graham's.

1977   Almost every-one; just beginning to come round and the lighter wines show considerable style. The Symington stable scored very highly this vintage, watch out for Gould Campbell and Smith Woodhouse; Fonseca and Taylor's are also good.

1980   Widely declared; medium to long term wines that are good value, again look out for Gould Campbell and Smith Woodhouse as well as Graham's and Warre's.

1982/3 Split between the lighter wines of 1982 and those with considerably more staying power from 1983. Some houses did not produce great wines and Croft in 1982 and Cockburn in 1983 are a little disappointing. Niepoort, Taylor's, and Graham's in 1983 are wines to keep.

Lock away, but don't lose the key!

1985   Universally declared; many needing another 10-15 years in the cellar, excellent wines from Fonseca, Graham's, Smith Woodhouse, Ferreira, and Offley.

1991/2 Another split declaration; big wines in both years, Churchill's, Dow's, Graham's and Warre's in 1991, and Taylor's and Fonseca in 1993 are good bets with both years coming round between 2005 and 2015.

1994   Widely declared; big intense wines with great potential and a long future. Unfortunately expensive due to the enormously increased interest in vintage port from the USA, nevertheless, these wines are a must for a serious collector.

A PERSONAL VIEW

I have long found Port to be the most seductive of wines; the silky smoothness and rich flavors of good port have always left me more satisfied than even the brilliance of top champagnes or the structured weight and elegance of the best Cabernets. There is little finer in the wine world than indulging oneself in the process of slowly decanting an old and treasured vintage port and sharing bottled history with a few friends.

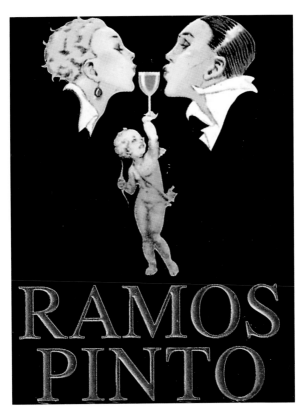

Today the packaging of port plays an important part in the promotion of the brand. This label is from Ramos Pinto's "Superior Tawny".

The moves towards promoting single quinta wines as expressions of the widely differing terroir in the Douro and the noble efforts of those producing elegant colheita wines should be applauded, both offer the port drinker value for money and, for some, a new direction in port drinking. As more and more export markets become interested in the finest wines, the allocations of vintage port will become smaller and therefore more expensive. The grand houses, already legendary through the development of the wine over the last three centuries, must keep their feet on the ground and maintain quality and innovation within the premium ruby and tawny markets where prices are more suited to the ordinary drinker.

Lastly it should always be remembered that good port is alive, it matures in the bottle and it needs to be kept well, cosseted, and drunk when in good condition. From personal experience, those treasured bottles of 1945, 1955, and 1963 in my own cellar do not always match the experiences described in other's tasting notes but never fail to engender lively discussion as to why!

The Wines

Borges

Owners: Sociedade dos Vinhos Borges e Irmao, SA
Established: 1884
Address: Av. da Républica, 796, Apartado 66,
4401 Vila Nova de Gaia Codex, Portugal
Vineyards: Quinta da Soalheira, Quintas da Junco,
and de Casa Nova

Once part of the very large commercial group of the same name, Borges are a big producer of port and wines from all over Portugal — more than a million cases each year! The company was unfortunately nationalized with its parent company in 1975, following the revolution, but has since been bought by its management under José Maria Vieira and is now looking to a bright future. 60% of the wines are exported, however only 2.5% are of vintage and colheita quality.

The company opened its lodge in Vila Nova at the beginning of this century and quickly followed that by buying the quintas at Junco and Soalheira. Quinta de Casa Nova was not added to the land holdings until 1926. Vinification is conducted at Junco and all of the company's premium wines are drawn from their own vineyards. The wines are all produced for early drinking, younger tawnies and are based on wines from Soalheira and Late Bottled Vintages and full Vintages from the vines at Junco.

Young wines aimed at the "value for money" market, are sold under the associated company of Garret & Ca. This house was set up in 1984 and the wines are recognizable for being bottled in short dump bottles, not at all suitable for ageing.

PRODUCE OF PORTUGAL

VINTAGE PORT
1994

BORGES
PORTO

PORTWINE GROWERS
PRODUCED AND BOTTLED BY
SOCIEDADE DOS VINHOS BORGES, S.A.
OPORTO-PORTUGAL

Burmester

Owners: J. W. Burmester & Co. Lda
Established: 1750
Address: Rua de Belomonte, 39-1
400 Porto, Portugal
Vineyards: Quinta Nova de Nossa Senhora do
Cormo

Burmester is another producer that developed from
a general trading company, and is still under family
control. Although the company has its offices in
Porto, the lodge is hidden deep in the heart of Vila
Nova de Gaia.

Traditionally, all of the grapes required were
bought in from contracted growers but recently, in
1991, the Gilbert Family, direct descendants of
Johann Wilhelm Burmester, purchased their own
vineyard holding at Nova de Nossa. This gives the
family just more than 100 acres (40 hectares),
planted only with the top five grape varieties,
which provides roughly a third of their requirements.

About 70% of their own wines are produced by
treading in lagares; the rest of the wines are made
from grapes bought from other farmers who have
sold to the family for decades. The major thrust of
the marketing lies behind the aged tawnies, which
are of excellent quality, but a full range is on offer.
The younger Jockey Club white and vintage character have been recently been repackaged with
modern labels and graphics.

Wines, especially old tawnies, are also sold
under the Gilberts label, a subsidiary company but
an existing house since 1914. These wines tend to
be sweeter than the occasional vintage declaration
also offered.

Cálem

Owners: A.A. Cálem & Filho, Lda
Established: 1859
Address: Rua de Reboleira, 7-4000
Porto, Portugal
Vineyards: Quinta da Foz, Quintas Sagrado, Santo
Antonio, and Vedial, amongst others.

Cálem are a large well-established company with diverse interests and have built up a considerable following for their ports. The company is managed by Ferrari driving Joaquim Manuel Cálem and his daughter Maria Assuncão.

Much is made of the vineyard holdings, eight farms in all providing 10% of the wine needed, and current vineyard development is well under way to increase productivity by replacing the older terraces with sloping patamares. When complete, this should allow for the production of almost 20,000 cases of A graded wine. The lodges hold in excess of 15,000 pipes of port.

At Quinta da Foz the grapes are still trod by foot and a single vintage Quinta wine is produced in lesser vintage years. Most of the company's wines are produced for early drinking and their Velhotes young tawny brand is the biggest seller within Portugal. Foz provides the basis for the vintage wines but in general the aged tawnies and colheitas are the best value wines. Wines are also marketed under the da Costa brand.

Cálem has one of the best suited lodges for visiting and offers guided tours of the maturation cellars which often lie below the level of the river when in full spate!

port

Churchill's

Owners: Churchill Graham Lda
Established: 1981
Address: Rua da Fonte Nova,5
4400 Vila Nova de Gaia, Portugal
Vineyards: No vineyards

The Churchill's brand of port is the most recent English port to be established, by Johnny Graham, following his departure from Cockburn's in 1981. With a long family heritage, through W. & J. Graham, Johnny Graham started his own company with the aim to produce high quality ports in a very traditional style. Unable, obviously, to use his own name he named the brand after his wife, Caroline Churchill.

To begin with the company rented a lodge from Taylor's, and found it quite difficult to get started. The quality of the first wines offered soon brought in the buyers and the future quickly became more attractive. As yet the company does not own any vineyards but buys in grapes from amongst others, excellent sites in the Pinhão — Quinta da Manuela and Quinta do Fojo — and the Douro at Quinta do Agua Alta.

Recent tastings have proved that the company has maintained the initial expectations of everyone in the trade and the vintage wines and single Quinta bottlings from Agua Alta have shown very well, especially the 1987 Agua Alta and the 1985 full vintage. Churchill also produces a traditional Late Bottled Vintage and crusted ports, which represent good value. One wine deserving of extra mention is the Dry Aperitif White, which has ten years ageing in old wood!

Cockburn's

Owners: Cockburn Smithes & Ca. SA
Established: 1815
Address: Ruas das Corados, 13, Apartado 20
4401 Vila Nova de Gaia Codex, Portugal
Vineyards: Quntas dos Canais and the Quintas do Tua, Atayde, and others.

Independent until 1962, the company was purchased by Harvey's of Bristol — famous for their sherry — and has since been incorporated into the Allied Domecq group thereby benefiting from all the advantages of belonging to one of the world's major wine and spirit producers.

Cockburn's is far and away the market leader in the UK, producing vary large quantities of reliable medium quality wines and the occasional top vintage and single quinta wine. Although they are owned by one of the world's largest wine and spirit combines, there have been family members involved throughout the years and top professional wine makers including Gordon Guimaraens, brother of Bruce at Fonseca.

Much of the wine is bought in from small growers in order to satisfy the volumes required for the Special Reserve Ruby and about 60% of their own quinta wines are still foot-trodden. Almost all the wine is made by pumping over, autovinification being considered too distant from the wine-makers' control.

Although quality is fully monitored by Cockburn's team of full-time winemakers, some recent vintage releases have not been as consistent as they should be and are perhaps lighter and for drinking sooner. The other wines to look out for are the Anno LBV and the Quinta do Tau vintage wines.

port

Croft's

Owners: Croft & Ca. SA
Established: 1678
Address: Largo de Joaquim Magalhães, 23,
Apartado 5
4401 Vila Nova de Gaia Codex, Portugal
Vineyards: Quntas da Roeda

One of the oldest of all port houses, the Croft Family was involved with trade to and from Portugal from the middle of the 17th century. The company established itself as one of the major shippers early in the 1800s, and in time developed markets throughout Europe and in the USA. In 1911, Croft's became one of the first houses to be bought by a large wine and spirit concern, Gilbey's, which through various take-overs and mergers has now evolved into Diageo, the world's largest wine and spirit producer and owner of brands such as Johnnie Walker Whisky and Gordon's Gin.

The finest wines come from the company's own quinta at Roêda, with the remaining being bought in from Ribalonga and Vale de Mendiz. Lagares are not used to any great extent due to the commercial pressures of producing large quantities of quality port and reliability rather than great quality is the watchword here.

Since 1992, the wines have been made by Nick Delaforce (who is also making the wines at sister company Delaforce) and the quality of the full vintage declarations have started to increase, but most wines are still for early drinking. Distinction Tawny has a fullish nose, a nut and spice palate, and the 10 and 20 year old tawnies are attractive if not of great length. The recently tasted 1983 Roeda, still widely available, was of full red color, fading to a brick red at the edge of the glass — quite mature with reasonable spice and a slightly short finish.

port

Delaforce

Owners: Delaforce Sons & Ca. — Vinhos Lda.
Established: 1868
Address: Largo de Joaquim Magalhaes, 23,
Apartado 6
4401 Vila Nova de Gaia Codex, Portugal
Vineyards: No vineyards

Founded by George Henry Delaforce, who had previously worked for Martinez Gassiot, the house of Delaforce has maintained family links with the company through various take-overs to the present day. The company is currently part of the IDV port stable alongside Croft's, and has good distribution through Europe and the USA.

All of the wines are bought in, although the company does have an exclusive contract with the Quinta da Corte vineyard that is sometimes bottled as a vintage single quinta offering. The Corte vineyard is a particularly good example of older walled terraces, which rise in quite dramatic fashion from the Rio Torto. The wines are made under the direction of Nick Delaforce, sixth generation of the founding family, and are generally light and elegant with the flagship tawny "His Eminence's Choice" being particularly fine.

Older vintages of Delaforce declared vintages, those prior to 1975, can represent very good value (especially the 1970 — a particularly full-bodied example of this great year) as does the recent Quinta da Corte 1991 which is full, soft, and ripe and at its peak quite soon.

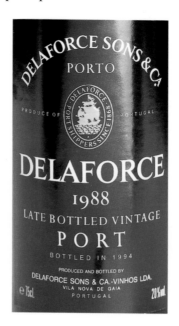

port

Dow's

Owners: Silva & Cosens Lda
Established: 1798
Address: Trav. Barão de Forrester, 85,
Apartado 192
4401 Vila Nova de Gaia Codex, Portugal
Vineyards: Quinta do Bomfim

Founded by a Portuguese merchant, Bruno da Silva, the name Dow's was not used until 1877 when James Dow became a partner. He was joined by Andrew Symington in 1912 and the company is now firmly in the Symington stable but has continued to be recognized for its own great strengths.

Dow's wines have always revolved round the superb Bomfin Quinta, purchased in 1890, which itself can produce the equivalent of 20,000 cases of wine, and operates as one of the main wineries for the whole group. A great percentage of the grapes are bought in, some from nearby quintas that the company has owned in the past, and now Dow's can also take advantage of the new Symington winery just across the valley, to process much of the volume required.

A full range of wines is offered including the AJS premium ruby, excellent 10 and 20 year old tawnies, crusted, and, since 1978, the vintage single quinta wines from Bomfin. Dow's wines can be slightly drier than the norm and the full vintages have a potential for many years ageing, often showing great concentration and depth which matures with a massive breadth of flavor. Classic vintages from Dow's are amongst the greatest wines from Portugal.

A recent tasting of Dow's ports in London showed examples right back through the last century and confirmed that many old wines from the twenties and thirties, and slightly unfashionable vintages such as 1966, are still drinking well.

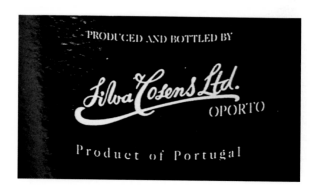

port

Feist

Owners: H & C J Feist — Vinhos SA
Established: 1836
Address: Rua D. Leonor de Freitas, 180/2,
PO Box 39
4401 Vila Nova de Gaia Codex, Portugal
Vineyards: Quinta da Fonte Santa

Founded by two German cousins working in London and Oporto, the Feist brand is now owned by the giant Barros, Almeida Company and like some other members of this group specializes in very old "colheita" tawnies.

A great deal of the wine is bought in, and both standard and full vintage wines are light in body and produced for early-drinking. Feist do however have access to the large Barros, Almeida library of vintage tawnies and many of the finest colheita wines are bottled under this label and can still be obtained back through the last 60 years.

A recently tasted 1991 vintage had all the hallmarks of a typical Barros wine: youthful purplish color and slightly dumb nose with good sweet flavors and a soft finish with no great length. Useful for current drinking.

Ferreira

Owners: AA Ferreira SA
Established: 1850
Address: 19/105 Rua da Carvalhosa
4400 Vila Nova de Gaia Codex, Portugal
Vineyards: Quinta do Porto and Quintas Seixo, da Leda and Caedo.

One of the giants of the port trade, Ferreira are the leading brand in Portugal and have been substantial vineyard owners and wine makers for many centuries. The backbone of the company was provided by the business acumen of Donna Antonia Adelaide Ferreira, the matriarch of the family for most of the 19th century. She was responsible for the majority of the vineyard purchases and built up an enviable stock of vines and wines. Quintas do Porto and Seixo lie in the Cima Corgo whilst da Leda is in the Douro Superior and features no terraces at all.

Now part of the Sogrape Group, owners of the Mateus Rose brand, the family is still involved with production and ensure that the reputation of the house is maintained. Much of the wine has to be bought in to satisfy the demands for quantity, but the quality remains good and many very fine wines are produced.

Good quality ruby under the Donna Antonia label and the Vintage Character wines are worth looking out, but special watch should be kept for the Quinta do Porto 10 year old tawny, the bench-mark tawny the Duke de Bragança 20 year old, and some recent full vintages which will repay keeping for more than 20 years.

Fonseca

Owners: Fonseca Guimaraens — Vinhos SA
Established: 1822
Address: Rua Barão de Forrester, 404, Apartado 13
4401 Vila Nova de Gaia Codex, Portugal
Vineyards: Quinta do Panascal, Quintas Santo
Antonio, and Cruzeiro

Although founded in Portugal, with the acquisition by Manoel Pedro Guimaraens of the merchant company Fonseca & Monteiro, Fonseca is very much an "English" port house in style and has been owned by the Taylor, Fladgate, Yeatman company since 1948. Amazingly, over the last century the wine making has been in the hands of only three members of the Guimaraens family and they have ensured that the reputation of the Fonseca wines has always been extremely high. David Guimaraens, the fourth in line, not only manages the vines here but also at Taylor's.

Grapes from the three class A quintas, a total of 174,000 vines, are still trodden by foot at Cruzeiro and the wines have a well structured style with plenty of finesse and grip. Vintage ports are declared in fine years, those labeled Fonseca Guimaraens in years which are not quite so outstanding, and Panascal is occasionally bottled as a single quinta. Special mention should be made of the standard ruby "Bin 27" which is an outstanding example and shows remarkable style and depth.

Lovers of huge powerful ports will find that Fonseca is a must for their cellars, especially the vintages from 1966 and 1977. Older vintages age remarkably well and the 1927, made by the current winemaker's grandfather, is still drinking well and shows all the legendary Fonseca staying power.

Gould Campbell

Owners: Smith Woodhouse & Ca, Lda
Established: 1797
Address: Trav. Barão de Forrester, Apartado 26
4401 Vila Nova de Gaia Codex, Portugal
Vineyards: Quinta de Santa Magdalena

Seemingly, enjoying a shared existence as one of the lesser known names under the massive umbrella of the Symington Group, Gould Campbell ports nevertheless still offer good quality and excellent value.

Unlike the major houses within the group, there appears to be no individual strategy for Gould Campbell but the wines do manage a consistent big full-flavored style. Over 90% of the grapes required are bought in; the rest coming from Santa Magdalena. Gould Campbell produces easy drinking modern ruby, Late Bottled Vintages, and some vintages which deserve rather more recognition and will age extremely well.

As the wines do not carry any premium prices and in years such as 1983, 1985, and 1991 the vintage wines are concentrated and full of plum fruit and vigor, the canny wine buyer will be assured of a bargain, even though he will have to wait as these are no early maturing wines.

**THE SEAL USED
BY MR. GARRETT GOULD TO BRAND
THE CASKS HE SHIPPED FROM OPORTO**

port

Graham's

Owners: W & J Graham & Co.
Established: 1820
Address: Trav. Barão de Forrester, 85, Apartado 19
4401 Vila Nova de Gaia Codex, Portugal
Vineyards: Quinta dos Malvedos

Established, originally as the trading outpost of a Scottish textile business, Graham's fell into the wine trade by swapping some bad debts for a few pipes of port. It is one of the great port brands and although it has a long connection with the Symington family, Andrew Symington having joined in 1882 only to leave soon after, it only became part of the group after falling on hard times in the late sixties.

Approximately 25% of the grapes come from Malvedos, mostly trodden by foot, and a great percentage of the rest is bought in from Quinta das Lages. Malvedos was bought in 1890 but by 1970 it was very run down and the Symingtons sold it, only to buy it back in 1982 and invest heavily in the vineyards and production infrastructure.

The wines produced are all big full flavored sweet wines with good length. The Six Grapes premium ruby and modern LBV are big sellers in both the UK and the USA and a single quinta style is produced under the Malvedos label in lesser years. The current releases of LBV, dated 1991 and 1992, have shown the Graham's style very well, with bright purple raspberry fruit, vigorous flavors and a spicy finish. Many outstanding full vintages have been produced over the last century and no serious collector of vintage ports would go without some Graham's in his cellar, particularly the 1945, 1963, and 1994 wines.

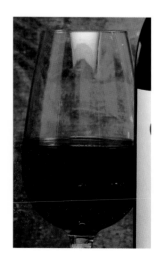

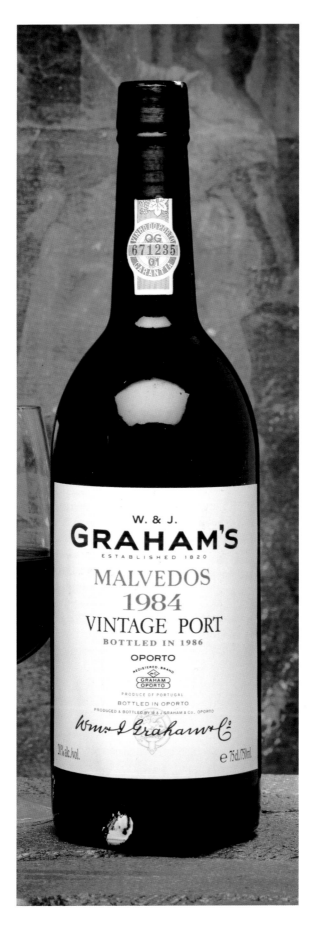

Hutcheson

Owners: Hutcheson, Feuerheerd & Associados Vinhos, SA
Established: 1881
Address: Rua D. Leonor de Freitas, 1802, PO Box 39
4401 Vila Nova de Gaia Codex, Portugal
Vineyards: Quinta da Santa Ana and Quinta de Dom Pedro

Founded as a port shipper rather than vine grower, by two English traders, the company has been in the hands of Barros, Almeida since 1927 and was amalgamated with the older company of Feuerheerd in 1996 along with Souza and other brands owned by the parent company.

Each of the companies has its own illustrious history, but unfortunately the finest vineyards were never kept and now the vast majority of grapes are bought in, current vineyard holdings are 300 acres (120 hectares). A full range of basic ruby, tawny, and white wines is offered under a large number of labels, with Souza specializing in colheitas, Hutcheson in ruby and vintage character, and Feuerheerd declaring vintages. On a rotational basis, most declared vintages can be found under one label or another and approximately 18% of the wines are colheita or vintage dated.

One of the giants of the port trade, the wines of Barros, Almeida, outside of the Feist and Kopke brands, tend to be light and aimed at the expanding markets of France and Belgium. They are, however, one of the few companies who have deliberately set up stockholdings of fine wines to be bottled as colheita vintages. These wines are laid down most years and bottled when required at ages up to 50 years old!

Also bottled under the Santos Junior, Vieira da Sousa, and Douro Wine Shippers labels. A total of one million bottles are sold each year, with 91% exported.

Kopke

Owners: C N Kopke & Ca, Lda
Established: 1638
Address: Rua D. Leonor de Freitas, 180/2,
PO Box 39
4401 Vila Nova de Gaia Codex, Portugal
Vineyards: Quinta São Luiz, Quintas Lobata, and
Mesquita

The oldest port house still in existence, Kopke was founded by Christiano Kopke, a German trader, and has been linked with another famous port family, the Van Zellers, several times through marriage and business links over the last three centuries.

Kopke still produce some excellent wines and although they are now owned by the ubiquitous Barros, Almeida, who purchased the company in 1953, a separate identity has been maintained.

The Quinta of São Luiz, in the heart of the Cima Corgo provides the finest A class grapes but more than 90% of the wines are bought in and modern technology has lead to an ever decreasing volume being trodden in favor of the pumping over process.

Although not widely distributed outside Europe, the wines do well in competition and have a reputation for sweetness and a firm body with the aged tawnies and colheitas representing the best selections.

port

Krohn

Owners: Wiese & Krohn, Sucrs., Lda
Established: 1865
Address: Rua de Serpa Pinto, 149, Apartado 1
4401 Vila Nova de Gaia Codex, Portugal
Vineyards: Quinta do Retiro Novo

Today, Weise & Krohn is an established Portuguese
house but the company was originally founded by a
two Norwegians of the same name who shipped
much desired salt cod to Portugal and port wines
back to Norway.

The quinta at Retiro Nova supplies only a very
small percentage of the wine needed by the
company and the rest are bought in either as grapes
to be vinified at the quinta, or as wine. As with
many houses, the same farmers have been supplying Weise & Krohn for the best part of this century.

The Krohns' style is especially suited to the aged
tawnies that they specialize in, but Iolande Carneiro
and Maria José Aguiar (two of the very few women
at the top of port production) also produce some
light and elegant vintages. Many of the older
colheitas are however extremely rich with a particularly sweet finish and are well worth searching
out.

the wines

port

Martinez

Owners: Martinez Gassiot & Co. Ltd
Established: 1790
Address: Rua Das Coradas, 13, Apartado 20
4401 Vila Nova de Gaia Codex, Portugal
Vineyards: Quinta de Eira Velha (under management)

Founded and run for almost 60 years by the Spaniard, Sebastian Martinez, the company was initially a trader in wines and cigars and was based in London. In 1822 Martinez was joined by an Englishman, John Peter Gassiot, and 12 years later a lodge was aquired in Vila Nova de Gaia to store the ever expanding stocks before bottling.

The company was purchased by Harvey's of Bristol in 1961 and, since 1962, has been run in conjunction with Cockburn's, although as a somewhat junior partner. The wines mainly come from the same vineyards as their sister company with the exception of the Quinta da Eira Velha, now managed by Martinez for the Newman family, and recently marketed as a single quinta wine. However much of the wine is matured at the Santa Maria lodge in Regua, where it develops a slightly sweeter and nuttier style.

From the large range of wines produced, including those under the Harvey's label, various sousmarques, and buyers-own-brands, the vintage character and vintage wines are particularly good and often represent remarkable value as they do not carry quite the same price as the Cockburn's wines.

Worth looking out for are: the Directors 20 year old Tawny, the 30 year old Tawny, and declarations from the 1994 and 1991 vintages for ageing as well as the 1970 and 1985 vintages which will be drinking for many years to come.

Messias

Owners: Sociadade Agricola E Comercial dos
Vinhos Messias SA
Established: 1926
Address: Rua Jose Mariani, 139, Apartado 66
4401 Vila Nova de Gaia Codex, Portugal
Vineyards: Qunta do Cachão and Quita do Rei

A traditional Portuguese family house, Senhor
Messias ran his port company for almost 50 years
before handing over to his sons who are also large
scale producers of table wines from Bairrada.

   Although they own two vineyards, these do not
supply anywhere near the company's requirements
so both grapes and wines are bought in. A wide
range of wines is produced, including a large
library of colheita vintages and some vintages
bearing the Cachão name. Most of the wines are
light and best drunk young, which has enabled the
company to establish a good trade in Europe with
aperitif style wines.

   A rather strange declaration policy has produced some slightly undistinguished vintages,
which are quick to mature and slightly lacking in
concentration.

Niepoort

Owners: Niepoort (Vinhos) SA
Established: 1842
Address: Rua Infante D. Henrique, 39-2
4050 Porto, Portugal
Vineyards: Quntas do Nopoles, Carril, and
Passadouro (in partnership)

A small Dutch house run by the founding family
since 1842. The current fifth generation, Dirk
Niepoort, has maintained the excellent reputation
of the company and continued in the traditional
methods that were established by five generations
of his ancestors.

As a wine-maker, Dirk Niepoort has also
established his own reputation and his wines are
very full bodied having both good balance and a
rich ripe structure which allows the wines to live at
their best for many years. The Niepoort philosophy
includes organic farming, as much foot treading as
possible, and the bottles also carry bottling dates,
thus giving the customer as much information
about the wine as possible. By allowing late ripen-
ing without losing the vital acidity, the wines have
the natural backbone which allows good ageing.

Very fine vintages such as 1955 and 1970 are
still developing and the traditional LBV is also well
worth searching out. Niepoort also specialize in
one of the dying styles of port, the Garrafeira selection — this is a wine which has been moved from
cask to glass demi-john to mature further before
being bottled and falls between an aged tawny and
a light vintage in weight.

Although the true gems of the Niepoort cellars
have always been the colheita vintage tawnies, all
the wines are worth looking out for especially by
those willing to put up with the long wait while
they develop in bottle.

port

Noval

Owners: Quinta do Noval — Vinhos SA
Established: 1813
Address: Avenida Diogo Leita, 256, Apartado 57
4401 Vila Nova de Gaia Codex, Portugal
Vineyards: Quinta do Noval

As a single quinta, this property has enjoyed a reputation second to none for the quality of its wines. Although the port has only been bottled and sold by the Quinta itself for the last 60 years, the wines previously commanded respect and top prices when sold to other houses.

Through the centuries, the owners of Noval have been responsible for many of the vineyard and terrace developments used throughout the region and the estate is a very visible landmark with its gently sloping terraces and whitewashed walls. Although the Van Zeller family is no longer involved — the current owner is a large French insurance company — innovation continues at Noval and they were the first estate to actually close their Vila Nova lodge in order to mature all their stocks in new air-conditioned cellars at the estate. They have also experimented with mechanical treaders to simulate the effect of foot treading.

The wines fall into two categories, those labeled simply Noval, which can be made with bought in grapes and those labeled with the Quinta name which are sourced only from the farm. The other exciting wines produced here, and greatly sought after by the cognoscenti, are the Nacional Vintages, which are produced from ungrafted vines grown in the oldest part of the vineyard — very rare and exceedingly expensive.

All of the wines are very well made, the rubies have a well structured sweetness, the tawnies have a dried fruit and nuts style, and the premium ruby Noval LB is excellent value. Full vintages are often huge, full flavored wines and very long lived, those from the late seventies and eighties were perhaps not quite as rich but the estate came right back to form with its 1991 and 1994 declarations.

port

Offley

Owners: Forrester & Ca., SA
Established: 1737
Address: Rua Guilherme Braga 38, Apartado 61
4401 Vila Nova de Gaia Codex, Portugal
Vineyards: Quinta do Boa Vista

Although the company is named after the Forrester Family, involved during the 19th century, the founder was William Offley from the West of England and to this day the wines still bear his name.

Currently owned by the Sogrape Group, (the brand has been also been owned both by Sandeman and the vermouth company Martini & Rosssi during the last 40 years) the main emphasis of production is based on quality tawnies and the single quinta vintages from Boa Vista, a vineyard of some 250 acres (100 hectares) in the Cima Corgo, between Régua and Pinhão.

The finest tawnies carry the "Baron de Forrester" name in memory of the famous cartographer and geographer of that name and the Duke of Oporto brand is well known in Portugal and Italy. Until recently all the declared vintages were sourced only from Boa Vista and although they were reasonably full-bodied and had good fruit they sometimes lacked the structure and backbone necessary for great wines.

Pocas

Owners: Manoel D. Pocas Junior — Vinhos S.A.
Established: 1918
Address: Rua Viscode das Devesas, 186,
4401 Vila Nova de Gaia Codex, Portugal
Vineyards: Quinta das Quartas, Quintas de Valde
Cavalos, and Santa Barbara

Pocas are one of the small number of Portuguese houses who have remained resolutely independent through thick and thin.

They have invested in both modern technology and a new ageing lodge in Vila Nova de Gaia and also age some of their tawnies at a lodge in the Duoro. The quintas they farm provide around 15% of the firm's requirements with a small proportion of these wines being foot trodden. The quintas themselves are picturesque with Quartas having the appearance of a very large and regimented walled garden.

The wines are sold under several names and, possibly partly due to their best markets, which are France and the Benelux countries, are designed for early drinking and as aperitifs. They tend to be very sweet and are often best drunk chilled. A small amount of old tawny is sold and since 1960 they have also declared some light and relatively easy drinking vintages.

Pocas wines are also available under the Pousada, Lopes, and Seguro labels.

port

Quarles Harris

Owners: Quarles Harris & Ca. S.A.
Established: 1680
Address: Trav. Barão de Forrester, 85,
Appartado 26
4401 Vila Nova de Gaia Codex, Portugal
Vineyards: No vineyards

Founded in 1680 and therefore one of the oldest shippers of port, Quarles Harrris became part of the giant Symington group, as a division of Warre's, but is seldom marketed with any great will.

The wines are made from grapes bought in by the parent company and tend to be less dense and slightly drier than those produced by their stable-mates. One advantage of the lack of brand awareness is that prices tend to be lower and the reliability conferred by membership of the Symington group means they should be good value. Perfectly correct winemaking will lead to good quality basic ruby and tawny wines and perhaps they and the vintages should be more widely available.

Perhaps not quite as good as the other second division ports from the Symington group, Quarles Harris have, in the last 20 years, declared good sturdy vintages with the 1980, 1983, and 1985 beginning to drink well and the 1991 and 1994 needing 10 to 15 years more ageing in bottle before they come round.

Quinta de la Rosa

Owners: Quinta de la Rosa — Vinhos Porto, Lda
Established: early 1900s
Address: Quinta de la Rosa, 5085 Pinhão, Portugal
Vineyards: Quinta de la Rosa

Established as a single property at the turn of the century by the Feuerheerd Family, the farm is an A grade property, and is still owned by their descendants, the Bergquists. The quinta was a big seller of wines to the other big houses, especially Sandeman, but when the export regulations changed in 1986 the wines were in less demand as bulk.

Since 1988, the family (who were concerned about the quality of wines being made from the grapes) have decided to develop the brand as a single quinta wine and have invested heavily in both the vineyards and the production plant. About 150,000 bottles can be produced each year with an emphasis on traditional qualities and production. Foot treading has been re-introduced and the wines are getting better and better.

This is definitely a property to look out for, particularly the 1991 Late Bottled Vintage and recent full declarations such as 1994. Well worth searching out and good value.

port

Quinta do Crasto

Owners: Sociedade Agricola da Quinta do Crasto
Established: 1910, as an independent producer
Address: Rua de Gondarém, 834 R/C Dt
4150 Porto, Portugal
Vineyards: Quinta do Crasto

Some 320 acres (130 hectares) make up this property, although only 48 are under vine, which produces red Douro wines as well as ports. The quinta belonged to Ferreira for many years, and the Almeida family since 1910 and it is currently owned by Jorge Roquette, who married into the Almeida Family.

The wines are made by David Baverstock, an Australian, who worked with the Symington Group for many years and the quinta also benefits from the experience of Christano van Zeller, formerly of Quinta do Noval. With such traditionalists at the helm it is not surprising that Crasto produces full bodied and potentially long lived wines. The older terraces have mixed plantings of different vines, some of which are up to 70 years old, and the newer patamares are planted by variety. A good part of the grape harvest is trodden in lagares the rest being produced by mechanical methods.

Currently only traditional LBVs and vintages are made but these show great potential and have good concentration. Around 15,000 cases are produced under the quinta name, the rest is sold in bulk to other shippers. Although vintage ports have been produced since 1927, they were for family consumption and the first commercial release was in 1978.

port

Quinta do Infantado

Owners: Quinta do Infantado, Lda
Established: 1816
Address: Rua Paulo da Gama, 550-8 E
4150 Porto, Portugal
Vineyards: Quinta do Infantado

One of the very first farms to sell and market their own wines and with a history that includes owner-ship by Portuguese royalty, Infantado has long been available on the Portuguese market, but like other quintas was only introduced to exports after the change in export rules in 1986.

The vineyard, situated in the Cima Corgo near Régua, has been divided into two with one part, named Serra, planted only with Touriga Nacional grapes for producing vintage wines and the other, named Barreiro, which is farmed organically. In the past the grapes have been bought by Taylor's and Sandeman's but the Roseira Family, who have owned the property since the turn of the century, now offer a complete range of wines.

Some well balanced traditional LBVs, aged tawnies and vintages have started to find their way out of Europe and with a little more consistency the wines will be well worth cellaring.

RUBY

SELECCIONADO entre as melhores colheitas de vinhos finos, tem uma venda limitada a fim de garantir a sua qualidade e todas as características dos vinhos generosos do Douro, restaurando assim a antiga tradição dos vinhos do Porto do Produtor.

port

Quinta do Vesúvio

Owners: Sociedade Agricola da Quinta do Vesúvio
Established: early 1800s
Address: Trav. Barão de Forrester, Apartado 26
4401 Vila Nova de Gaia Codex, Portugal
Vineyards: Quinta do Vesúvio

Almost 1,000 acres (400 hectares) of premium A rated vineyards! This is one of the most outstanding vineyards in the whole region and was owned by the Ferreira family from 1823 until 1989 when it passed into the control of the ubiquitous Symington Group. However, unlike the other quintas under their control, Vesúvio has been established as an independent shipper.

Considerable investment has taken place at the estate with maturation and bottling taking place on site. Amazingly, all of the wines are produced in lagares, and the vintages that have been declared show extremely well as medium to long term wines with a deep soft opulent style.

Vesúvio is now declared as a vintage when the grapes are outstanding; in poor years, the wines will be used by other members of the group or sold on to other companies. Almost 40,000 bottles of vintage port can be produced in good years and the wines are destined to become an important part of any port collector's cellar.

As a portent for the future, this type of quinta may be the forerunner of limited bottlings at premium quality and price that the market may see from other companies as well.

Ramos Pinto

Owners: Adriano Ramos Pinto (Vinhos) S.A.
Established: 1880
Address: Av. Ramos Pinto, 380, Appartado 1320
4401 Vila Nova de Gaia Codex, Portugal
Vineyards: Quintas Bom Retiro, São Domingos,
Ervamoira, Urtiga, and Bons Ares (for Douro wine)

Ramos Pinto, which was founded with the aims of
exporting to Latin America, has developed into a
large vineyard owner, and one of the most innova-
tive of port companies with modern wineries and
computer controlled production. The winemaking
is still run by descendants of the family, although
control lies with the Champagne house Louis
Roederer.

The company is also at the forefront of vine
development and vineyard management, with the
best clonal varieties planted, and at Ervamoira not a
terrace to be seen anywhere! Very few grapes are
bought in and the best varieties are still foot-trodden every year, with the current manager João
Nicolau de Almeida, a direct descendent of the
house's founder, managing to brilliantly balance
traditional methods and modern technology.

Ramos Pinto is one of the few companies to
aggressively market their wines using the quinta
names and is famous for the quality of the aged
tawnies, 10 year old from Ervamoira, 20 year old
from Bom Retiro, and also a premium ruby from
Urtiga. Full vintages are also declared but seldom
reach the heights of the aged tawnies and although
fragrant and delicate are for early drinking.

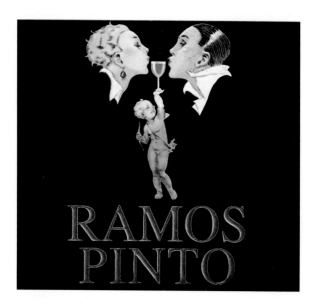

Royal Oporto

Owners: Real Companhia Velha Lda.
Established: 1755
Address: Rua Azevedo Magalhaes, 314
4430 Vila Nova de Gaia Codex, Portugal
Vineyards: Quintas Carvalhas, Aciprestes, Casal da
Graja, Sidro, and others.

A collection of companies, including one founded
by order of King Jose I, the company grew enormously from the 1950s, under the aegis of one man,
Manuel Silva Reis, but since 1974 has suffered many
setbacks. After the revolution, that year, the company was nationalized and the vast majority of its
best stock was sold off to other port companies.

Following its sale back into private hands,
control has passed through several hands and
controversy continues to dog the company. In
1990, 40% of the company was purchased by the
Casa do Duoro, one of the modern day regulatory
bodies for the industry. Unfortunately, today it is
very difficult to combine any regulatory duties
when the *raison d'etre* of a commercial company is
profitability and the other shippers were naturally
suspicious that the company could combine its
functions.

Nowadays the Casa do Duoro has lost much of
its power and the Real Companhia Velha, although
the largest landowner and with obvious potential,
produces mainly light rubies and tawnies for early
drinking under a myriad of different brands such as
Pitters, Hooper, Silva Reis, and Souza Guedes.
Vintages are frequently declared and again are best
in their youth when they are sweet and vigorous.

Rozès

Owners: Rozès Lda
Established: 1855
Address: Rua Candido dos Reus, 526/532,
Apartado 376
4401 Vila Nova de Gaia Codex, Portugal
Vineyards: Quinta do Monsul

Founded by a Bordeaux trader, Ostende Rozès, this was the only port house established by the French and is currently owned by the massive LVMH multinational — owners of Moët & Chandon Champagne and Hennessy Cognac — after the family relinquished control in 1974.

The company owns one of the oldest quintas at Monsul, but this contributes less than 1% of the grapes Rozès needs. The rest are bought in from top quality vineyards with the finest grapes being crushed in the lagares and the rest going into tanks for pumping over. Wine, has in the past been supplied by Taylor's and Ferreira, but the company is now building stocks for the future at the lodge in Vila Nova de Gaia.

The wines tend towards the lighter more elegant end of the port spectrum but always have good balance and are particularly well suited to the young tawny aperitif style required by the French owners.

port

Sandeman

Owners: Sandeman & Ca. SA
Established: 1790
Address: Largo de Miguel Bombarda, 3, Apartado 2
4401 Vila Nova de Gaia Codex, Portugal
Vineyards: Quinta do Vau

Renowned for the Don silhouette logo on the label, the company was founded by George Sandeman from Perth in Scotland, in 1790, and rapidly became a major force in both the port and sherry markets. Over the next century, Sandeman became the largest shipper with almost 10% of the export market.

By concentrating on buying in grapes, Sandeman was able to avoid the pitfalls of land ownership and the vineyard problems of turn of the century and continued to motor ahead in the volume market. In fact the quinta at Vau produces less than 1% of the company's requirements. Having bought and sold Offley Forrester during the sixties and seventies, Sandeman itself became part of the Seagram Group, in 1980, and with the distribution advantages this gave, soon became the world's biggest brand.

Wines not trodden by foot are made by autovinification and the resultant ports are youthful and full-flavored and quite early to mature. The single Quinta do Vau is worth looking out for and the vintages tend to be quite good value but without the depth and breadth that they had prior to 1970. Partners Ruby and Imperial Tawny perform well in many markets and the revitalized Founder's Reserve is a leading brand in America.

The company also controls Robertson, which sells wine under the Rabello Valente brand.

Smith Woodhouse

Owners: Smith Woodhouse & Ca., Lda
Established: 1784
Address: Trav. Barão de Forrester, 85, Apartado 19
4401 Vila Nova de Gaia Codex, Portugal
Vineyards: uses grapes from Quinta Santa
Madalena

Founded by Christopher Smith, an Englishman who
could claim not only to have been a Member of
Parliament but who also went on to be Lord Mayor
of London.

Smith Woodhouse was purchased by Graham's
early this century, and then became part of the
Symington Group when Graham's in its turn was
purchased by them. The brand maintains a separate
identity and produces many excellent and
frequently under-rated vintages: the 1977 and 1983
are both superb wines.

The company produces many different styles of
wines, some under buyers' own brand labels, and
has established a separate market for rather old
fashioned late-bottled vintages which are unusually
bottled without filtering after four years in cask.
This wine will mature further in the bottle and is
released when ready for drinking, up to 10 years
later, and needs decanting before drinking.

Smith Woodhouse wines have rarely disappoint-
ed me, and as they are normally sold at prices well
under those of their more illustrious stable-mates.
Not only are they good value, they often have a very
long life and although more often comparable to
Warre's in style, in the seventies and eighties they
have been a perfect marriage of sweetness and
strength.

Taylor's

Owners: Taylor, Fladgate & Yeatman — Vinhos SA
Established: 1692
Address: Rua do Choupelo, 250, Apartado 1311
4400 Vila Nova de Gaia Codex, Portugal
Vineyards: Quinta de Vargellas and Quinta de Terra Feita

Century after century the Taylor's wines have been amongst the very best of ports, and one vineyard bought in 1744 still remains in Taylor's ownership. Although the firm has changed its name occasionally, it has never been bought, sold, or taken over and the present arm of the family date back to the early 19th century. Taylor's is still resolutely independent and with the purchase of Fonseca in the 1940s it has secured its position in the forefront of port production.

Grapes from the two A graded quintas are all foot trodden in the lagares, but large quantities of top rated grapes are also bought in to satisfy the demands of quantity. The company has been managed by Alistair Robertson for the last 30 years and it is he who has masterminded the development of the house and its branded premium ruby and LBV wines.

Always famed for its vintage wines, based round the Vargellas vineyard, Taylor's also produce an excellent premium ruby called First Estate, rich tawnies and a remarkably consistent LBV. The hallmarks of Taylor's vintages; a huge depth, structure, and concentration of fruit are ideal for long lived wines and the vintages such as 1927, 1948, and 1963 produced true classics which are still drinking. For those who cannot afford the full vintages, the single Quinta offerings from both Vargellas and Terra Fieta offer a similar style at much less of the cost. Due to the large selection of fine old wood ports held by the house a 40 year old Tawny is also available.

The company is also active in the buyers-own-brand market and through its own sales and those of Skeffington, a sister company, supplies many quality ruby and vintage character wines.

port

Vista Alegre

Owners: Vallegre — Vinhos do Porto SA
Established: 1973
Address: Rua Sporting Clube Coimbroes,
Apartado 101
4401 Vila Nova de Gaia Codex, Portugal
Vineyards: Quinta de Vista Alegre, Quinta de Valonga, Quinta de Vilarinho, and Quinta da Lamaeira

Vista Alegre is the principal brand belonging to Vallegre, the marketing arm of the old established family company, Sociada Agricola Barros. The company, although formalized only in 1973, has been a vineyard owner and wine producer for five generations through the founding family.

The company is based wholly in the Douro at Quinta de Vista Alegre and they use traditional lagares as well as pumping over. The quintas supply more than 70% of the company's requirements and the wines are stored on site for maturation.

A large range of wines is marketed including 10, 20, 30, and 40 year old tawnies, LBVs from 1991 and 1994, and a full vintage from 1994. Unlike many quinta-based companies, the company is yet to market its wines under individual quinta names.

Warre's

Owners: Warre & Ca., SA
Established: 1670
Address: Trav. Barão de Forrester, 85, Apartado 26
4401 Vila Nova de Gaia Codex, Portugal
Vineyards: Quinta de Cavadinha

The oldest British port house, Warre's was involved in wine trading for its first 50 years, before moving to Oporto and settling into the port trade. The Warre family was heavily involved in the trade and in the organization of the British shippers, to the extent of designing and building the Factory House (the "club" for British Shippers in Oporto) where regulatory problems could be discussed in private.

The Warre Company became, in 1905, the stepping stone to an empire for Andrew Symington and his descendants. Following a share swap with the Warre Family to take control of Silva & Cosens (the producer of Dow's), Quarles Harris was bought and then the Warre family bowed out as a shareholder in the group in the 1960s, leaving the fourth generation of Symingtons in charge. Throughout the centuries, however, the wines have always shone and more than half is of premium quality showing great power and structure.

Winemaking is currently centered on Cavadinha and Bonfim, with up to 25% of the wines being foot-trodden. The aptly named Warrior Reserve Ruby, the Cavadinha single Quinta and declared full vintages are particularly worth looking out for. One must also mention the bottle-matured Late Bottle Vintage, similar in style to Smith-Woodhouse, and released when mature for drinking.

Warre's is also active in the French markets with lighter tawny styles sold under the Cintra brand.